A Cat with Four Paws

by Jake Walker

Harcourt

Orlando   Boston   Dallas   Chicago   San Diego

Visit *The Learning Site!*

www.harcourtschool.com

A cat has four paws.
Can you see the paws?

2

A pig has a curly tail.
Can you see the tail?

3

A turtle has a hard shell.
Can you see the shell?

4

An elephant has a long trunk.
Can you see the trunk?

A rabbit has whiskers.
Can you see the
whiskers?

A lion has a furry mane.
Can you see the mane?

A lobster has two claws.
Can you see the claws?

8

A deer has a set of
antlers.
Can you see the antlers?

A camel has a large
hump.
Can you see the hump?

A giant panda has black
and white fur.
Can you see the fur?

A kangaroo has a deep pouch.
Can you see the pouch?